Managing Anger Successfully

Managing Anger Successfully

Charles Confer

Writers Club Press
San Jose New York Lincoln Shanghai

Managing Anger Successfully

Writers Club Press
an imprint of iUniverse.com, Inc.

For information address:
iUniverse.com, Inc.
620 North 48th Street
Suite 201
Lincoln, NE 68504-3467
www.iuniverse.com

ISBN: 0-595-12030-X

Printed in the United States of America

PREFACE

I see you have picked up this book and that you are looking at it. Good!

Now, I ask you a question: "Why should you read this book? What's in it for you? What are you going to get out of it?"

Take a quick look at the two following examples of how a parent might handle a teen's angering behavior and then decide if you want to read further.

Example One

P = Parent and T = Teenager

P1 Going out? Be home at 11:00. OK?

T1 11:00? You must be kidding. No one comes home at 11:00 anymore.

P2 Well, maybe no one else comes home at 11:00 o'clock, but you are!

T2 There you go again. Giving orders. I might as well be in a boot camp as live in this house.

P3 A boot camp is where you'll be living if you don't watch your attitude.

T3 Threats! Threats! Yeah, you wish I'd be out of here, but Mom won't let you even touch me. You know that and I know that. You can't do anything to me.

P4 Let your mother out of this or you will be in deep problems, buddy, and I'm serious.

T4 Yeah. You and whose army? You touch me and I'll call on the Abuse Hotline so fast that your head will spin.

P5 Talk about threats. Think you're a big man but yet you got to call the Child Abuse Hotline. Get it, buster, the "Child" Abuse Hotline because that's what I'm dealing with here, a child.

T5 I'm out of here, and I'll be back when I get good and ready, and you can't do anything about it. (Leaves the house.)

P6 Yeah. Well, we'll see. You gotta come back here sometime, big man; and when you do I'll still be here and you'll have to deal with me. Sooner or later you're gonna get yours.

Example Two

P1 Going out? Be home at 11:00. OK?

T1 11:00? You must be kidding. No one comes home at 11:00 anymore.

P2 I thought we had agreed on 11:00 for Friday nights because you have soccer practice early Saturday.

T2 Yeah. Agreement. If that's what you call it. I call it more like living in a prison camp. You're always on my case. Do this. Do that. Always bringing up that agreement stuff. Why don't you just take care of yourself and I'll take care of myself?

P3 Yes. You're right. I am on your case sometimes.

T3 I'd say more than sometimes. You're on my case about what time I come home, my friends and my grades. You always gripe about my grades.

P4 You're right. I am concerned about your grades.

T4 Well, why don't you spend some of your time worrying about Mark? Wow! Just because he's seventeen you let him do everything he wants. Why aren't you on his case, too? Just because he's three years older than I am he can do anything.

P5 Right. Mark is seventeen. You're right.

T5 He's so much of a jerk. You don't know half the stuff he does. But I do. If you knew as much as I do about what Mark does you would be on his case, too.

P6 You're right, Kevin, I don't know everything that Mark does.

T6 Well, I'm just getting tired of perfect Mark being allowed to do whatever he wants and you and Mom being on my case all the time.

P7 Well, Kevin, how would you like it to be? What changes would you make around here?

T7 Everyone would get off my back.

P8 OK, what would be different if we, as you say, got off your back?

T8 I don't know exactly. I could do more of what I want.

P9 Your mother and I want you to get as much of what you want as is possible. What would you change in order to get more of what you want?

T9 I'd stay out all night and come in when I want to.

P10 Do you really think that will fly here in this household?

T10 Nah. You would never allow that I guess.

P11 Yep, you're right. Staying out all night won't fly. So what else would you change?

T11 I don't know. But I hate coming in at 11:00 when everyone else stays until 11:30.

P12 So we're talking about a half an hour here?

T12 I know it seems small potatoes to you. But it's important to me.

P13 OK. It's important. I have a concern because when you come home even at eleven o'clock, you don't go to bed until much later. And then I have a dickens of a time getting you up for soccer practice at nine in the morning. You see my point?

T13 Yeah.

P14 So what do you think we could do to not have you feel odd man out at the teen center and yet meet my needs not to have a complete furor in the morning before you go to soccer.

T14 But I like to sleep in on Saturday morning.

P15 Yep. Sleeping in is fun. I'm wondering what you want to do: Sleep in or play soccer?

T15 Oh, I guess I want to play soccer. No, I know I want to play soccer. But sometimes it's a pain in the neck to get up to go to practice. But if I don't go to practice, I can't play in the game.

P16 You're right. No practice. No game. What do you want to do about it all?

T16 Do you suppose if I came home at 11:30 and went straight to bed that that would work.

P17 After a late snack, but no television? Is that what you're saying?

T17 Yep. What do you think?

P18 11:30 home, snack and off to bed? Sounds OK to me as long as we can avoid that ramming around in the morning before soccer.

T18 OK then. Let's write it on a Post-It and put it on the bulletin board like we did with our plan for the chores.

P19 OK with me. You write it. I'll sign it.

T19 Jeez, Dad, you're always looking for ways to get out of work.

P20 Yep. If I can get you to write it, I'm a happy dad.

T20 What are parents coming to anyhow?

P21 Beats me. Now write that agreement so I can sign it.

If you want to learn or teach these skills, I believe this book just might be the one for you.

FORWARD

I am writing this book for you. You may be a parent, a counselor, a partner in marriage or a youth worker. Perhaps you are a teen, a student, or a teacher/trainer. Maybe you are a manager, a supervisor or a community leader. I am writing this book for anyone who in his or her personal or professional life must deal with anger.... his own anger or the anger of another person.

After reading this book, I trust you will have gained knowledge and skills in three areas. The first is an understanding of the dynamics of angry behavior; the second is having skills and insights to manage both your own anger and the anger of another person. Thirdly, you will know how to keep anger from damaging personal and professional relationships.

In this book I have borrowed much from the thinking, experiences and writings of teachers, colleagues and clients. I take full responsibility for the ordering and presentation of the material.

I do wish to express my appreciation to those special people who made this book possible. William Glasser, who developed Reality Therapy and Choice Theory psychology, has been my teacher since I first read *Reality Therapy* in the library of the University of Pittsburgh Graduate School of Social Work in

1965. I urge everyone to read Dr. Glasser's *Choice Theory* and *Reality Therapy in Action*. Simply put, they are the two most helpful books on counseling I have ever read.

I acknowledge my gratitude to Mary Lotspeich, my closest colleague. Mary has helped me develop and implement anger management skills both in our family relationships and in our practice of social work. Also, I owe thanks to the thousands of colleagues, clients, students, children and youth workers and foster parents who through the years have helped to shape my thinking and practice of professional social work.

I owe a special thanks to Wendall Walker Senior Faculty Instructor of the William Glasser Institute who spent hours pouring over this manuscript and for offering support, encouragement and many helpful, important suggestions.

Before we get into the details of anger management, I want to present a general overview of what will be coming in the pages ahead. As a therapist, I approach a person who is "angering" (angering is a behavior, an action word, so let's use the word in a verb form) with four ideas in my mind. These ideas are like psychological "light houses" which guide me in my work with the client, his problems and conflicts.

The first idea may seem too obvious: Angering is a behavior. Angering is something that the client does. You can see angering. Angering has an identity and a force. The behavior might be yelling, hitting, swearing, driving like a maniac, hurting, sulking, pouting, arguing, drunking, disobeying...or whatever-ing. So, the first thing I do in assessing a client's situation is to identify what he is doing. What behaviors is the client demonstrating? How is she expressing her anger?

Second: Angering is a behavior the client chooses. No person or thing can "make" the client be or do anything. The client is responsible for the behaviors she chooses, and sometimes the behavior the client chooses in an attempt to make his life more satisfying is anger. Of course, if the client chooses to anger, the client is also free to choose other non-angering behaviors. And helping the client choose non-angering behaviors is one of my goals in counseling. The client is responsible for making behavioral choices and living with the consequences of those choices even though she may try to avoid his responsibility by blaming someone or something else.

Third: Angering usually has something to do with a relationship that has gone awry. If the client's relationships at school, in the family or at work are satisfying, the less chance there is for angering in his life. If the client's personal relationships are damaged and she is "disconnected" from an important person (parents, teachers, bosses, spouse) angering may result. Thus, in an initial assessment of the angering person's situation, I always look at the health of his important personal relationships.

Fourth: When you meet an angering person you can be sure of this: Some where in the angering person's life there is a conflict. When a client angers, I can be certain there is someone in the client's life who is trying to make the client do something she doesn't want to do…or the client is trying to make someone else do something that person does not want to do…or the client is trying to make himself do something he does not want to do. In my initial assessment, I ask the question: Where is the conflict? Who is trying to make whom do what? Who is using manipulative coercion in this client's life?

So much for the introduction, now let's get down to business. The first item on the agenda is to explore the question: What is anger? And why do people choose such behavior as angering in the first place?

CHAPTER I
What is Anger And Why Do People Choose Angering Behavior?

Anger is a common, every day experience. I am sure you in your lifetime have angered at least "once or twice" and have certainly witnessed others who regularly anger. All of us have known angering people who at one time or another have shouted, hit, stomped, thrown and broken things, driven vehicles recklessly, belittled others, criticized, punched holes in walls, blamed others, hurt people or animals, destroyed property, sulked, pouted, became red in the face, tensed body muscles, raged and yelled, fired guns….just to note a few angering behaviors.

My dictionary defines anger as a strong feeling of displeasure and belligerence, wrath or ire. Anger also implies fury, rage and indignation. The dictionary states that "anger" is a noun and also a verb, an action word. Anger can be correctly used as a verb in a sentence such as this: "Will angering when the teacher corrects your mistakes help you to get a better grade?" Or, "Dad sure angered when that guy cut in front of him out there on the Freeway." Although this usage may seem strange and awkward,

1

throughout this book we will continue using anger in a verb form wherever appropriate. And I invite you to experiment with using "anger" as a verb and not only as a noun.

The word "anger" is an ancient word. It came into the English language about a thousand years ago from the Scandinavian and Old Norse languages. Angering must have been what the English experienced when they saw those long ships sailing in from the North Sea loaded with Vikings who were ready for pillage and plunder.

Angering is also an ancient behavior; by this I mean people learn how to anger at a very early age. Angering is the basic skill a baby soon learns after birth in order to survive and be fed and cared for. Anyone who has had a newborn child in the home knows what I am talking about: When the baby is hungry or wants to be picked up and held or have its diaper changed what does it do? The baby tenses itself, makes itself rigid and red in the face and yowls at the top of its lungs. Sounds like the picture of an angering person to me.

I suggest that anger may be experienced in two stages: Flash Anger and Choice Anger. Flash Anger is that sudden, strong sense of displeasure that seems to "just happen" when something goes radically "wrong" in life. Flash Anger takes place unexpectedly! You are driving on the Interstate and suddenly, without warning a guy/gal in a flashy SUV passes you and cuts in right in front of you. You could easily experience "Flash Anger." You may have the urge to tailgate or flash a hand signal to the other driver; or you may simply feel your blood pressure rise fifty points. Flash Anger is unpredictable and unexpected; it just seems to come out of nowhere like a "bolt out of the blue." However, if you are still angering 10 seconds after the onset of "Flash Anger" you are then choosing your angering behavior; you have moved from "Flash Anger" to "Choice Anger." We will discuss this notion of angering as a behavioral choice thoroughly later; but for the time being, I want you to become familiar with the idea that angering not only "just happens" as flash anger but also that angering is a "chosen" behavior.

Common knowledge tells us that "anger" is merely an emotion, a feeling: "Oh, I am feeling so angry I could spit nails." "Every time he lies to me I feel so angry." However, I would like you to consider the notion that angering is a "total behavior" which embodies and integrates what a person does, thinks, feels and his/her physical self.

The doing component of total behavior is composed of our actions: Running, writing, crying, yelling, throwing, skiing, swimming, running, lifting weights, throwing spit balls, reading, visiting, walking, playing the piano and the list goes on. The thinking component of our behavior is always busy. Some of the thoughts we may have are planning what to cook for supper, wondering if the teacher likes me, knowing that I have to do my homework before I can watch television, figuring arithmetic problems, working out how to write a book, considering what to do this weekend with my friends or wondering what I should wear today. Our emotions serve us as "signals" which alert us to what is going on inside of us; we are generally aware when we experience strong emotions, feelings such as anger, love, hate, fear, sadness and joy. And the last component of total behavior is physiology. One is not always aware of what is going on inside the body, but without that physical activity the body will die: The heart beating, lungs breathing, the stomach digesting and breaking food into usable fuel, the operation of neurotransmitters in the brain, muscles flexing are parts of physiology.

The notion of total behavior is an important component of anger management. Total behavior is an integrated system and when one element of total behavior is changed, there are shifts and changes in the other elements. If I were to get up out of the chair I am sitting in and walk down the steps to the kitchen (a change in my doing behavior), there would certainly be changes in what I am thinking, in what I am feeling and in my physiology. Total behavior is similar to an algebraic equation in that when you change a factor on one side of the equal sign, there will be changes on the other side of the equal sign. As you will see later, this notion is important when we explore what steps can be taken to manage angering. It is enough to say at this point that if a person who is angering changes one part of his total behavior, there will be changes in the other parts of her total behavior.

Now let us proceed to the second question: Why do people choose anger? At first glance in light of "common sense" you might respond, "I don't choose anger. People or things outside of me make me angry." This is what most people maintain when they come into my office for counseling; they initially disagree with me that angering is a chosen total behavior. And they also mistakenly believe that externals such as people and events that are outside them, even things that have happened in their lives years ago, have the power to control their lives and actions.

For a moment, let us consider an alternative explanation of why people behave the way they do. For a full exploration of this issue, I refer you to Dr. Glasser's book, *Choice Theory: A New Psychology of Personal Freedom*.

Instead of thinking of human behavior as something that is controlled by external forces, let us experiment with the notion that individuals have within them the drive and the ability to choose their behaviors and that these choices are purposeful and logical. An individual chooses behaviors in order to make life more satisfying, to achieve more enjoyment, increase pleasure and to avoid pain and suffering. Instead of being motivated by "externals," I am suggesting that you and I and all other human beings are born with psychological as well as physical directives in our DNA. Each living person has within his/her DNA vast amounts of information that will determine what he or she will physically become. I have the genetic instruction to have brown eyes, fair skin and grow to five feet and nine inches tall. You have your own set of genetic instructions that will largely determine your physical self. I am suggesting in addition to the DNA that determines ones physical self there is also genetic material that determines ones psychological self, too. People are born with genetically driven needs such as survival and the psychological needs for power, love and belonging, freedom and fun. And all through life we have experienced people, places, things and systems of beliefs, which have satisfied or not satisfied these needs. We have stored in our minds the pictures of the need meeting people, things and events. These pictures make up a person's Quality World, a personal-what-I-want-to-happen-in-my-life world. The Quality World contains the pictures of the way one would like things to be in his or her Real World where she lives, loves, works and plays. In my Quality World, I have pictures of my wife, family and friends where we are healthy and happy and get along reasonably well with each other. I have a picture of our home and my 1992 Ford Taurus that sits in the driveway, completely payment free. I have a picture in my mind of finishing this book. And I see myself getting off an airplane at London Heathrow where my friends are waiting to greet me. I see myself walking to my friend's house for a cup of tea this afternoon. These pictures are just a glimpse of the millions of pictures that I have placed in my Quality World.

Each person fills his or her Quality World with innumerable pictures of how he or she would like the Real World to be. But often there is a conflict between what a person wants in the Quality World and what he or she is receiving in the Real World. When this painful conflict occurs, a person may experience Flash Anger and then choose angering to remedy the situation and eliminate or at least reduce the conflict. He or she chooses angering because angering is the best thing she knows to make the Real World more like his Quality World. It may seem strange, but a person chooses angering because she believes the angering behavior will create a more satisfying life and make things in his Real World more the way he wants them to be.

It is interesting that most people who come to me for counseling believe something or someone outside them has the power to make them angry. They describe relationships with children or spouses by saying, "He knows exactly what buttons to push to set me off." Or, "When she doesn't support me, she makes me so very angry." Here again are examples of the choice theory psychology vs. the external control psychology question. I remind people that things and objects have no power to make choices: Elevators have buttons and people push the buttons to get the elevator to take them up or down; the elevator has no choice in the matter. People are not elevators. People do not have buttons that make them behave; some external force, person or thing does not control people.

Instead of external forces manipulating us, you and I, our children, our colleagues, our clients, our customers…all of us choose total behaviors (doing, thinking, feeling and physiology) with one purpose, one focused goal. That goal is to meet needs and to make life more satisfying…to make the real world look more like the pictures that we have stored in our personal Quality World.

But you ask, "IF people choose their behaviors and IF their behaviors are logical and reasonable, WHY would anyone choose angering to make his or her world more satisfying? How can angering meet an individual's psychological needs for power, love and belonging, freedom and fun?"

People choose angering behavior because it works. Anger is powerful. And many people have chosen anger as a way to meet their needs for survival, power and freedom.

First: Anger sends a very clear "PAY ATTENTION TO ME!!!" message. Many have learned that when they are not getting the attention they desire if they anger things will start happening and people probably will begin paying attention. Anyone with a newborn baby in the house knows all about this. The same behavior of angering to get attention can also be seen in adults. For an example, when I am listening to a client in a counseling session and she is angering on about how much she does for other people and how no one appreciates what she does, I ask: "Who's not listening to you?" And I usually get the answer.

Second: Human beings use angering as a means of trying to control situations and other people. Angering is a powerful behavior and is used by many to get more of their Quality World active in the Real World. Some teachers try to control their students 'behaviors through angering. Parents have used angering to control the conduct of the children. Even the teenagers I see for counseling have been known to use anger in order to manipulate the behaviors of others in the family or at school. Haven't you at least once in your life chosen to change your behavior in light of angry threats, heated warnings, browbeating or loud cursing and bullying? You see, angering works.

Third: Avoidance. People choose angering as a means of escaping from doing things they don't want to do. Last week a lady was in my office and she was furious at her husband. She irritated on about his not treating her right and not paying attention to her; he just watched TV or read the newspaper every night, and she was irating. However, the longer I allowed her to go on venting her anger, the less willing she was to examine her part in the disconnectedness that has taken place in the marriage relationship. Her situation was not unlike the 8th grader who was explosive about the school, the teachers, and the horrible meals they served in the school cafeteria. The longer he went on about how terrible things were at school, the longer he could avoid seriously examining the problems he was causing for himself by not doing his homework, not studying for tests and not paying attention in class.

Fourth: People who feel small and inadequate sometimes choose angering behavior to pump themselves up. Being the "outsider" in the group of youth or adults is often an uncomfortable position. You get picked on and belittled. You are made the butt of jokes. In school, your locker gets wrecked and others make fun of you. However, angering can provide some "equalization" if other people perceive that their security and safety may be endangered by your crazy, violent angering behavior. Unfortunately, in the United States, we have recently witnessed too much of this type of angering especially with the use of firearms in the public schools and on the college campuses.

Angering gets results; it is a powerful behavior. However, in every act of angering, usually blame and criticism are communicated. When an individual angers at another person a subtle message is spoken: "I am angry. It is your fault. You have done something wrong or bad to make me feel this way, and you should feel guilty and change your behavior immediately." Needless to say, this powerful message can do serious damage to relationships.

So then, the question arises: Is angering always bad? Not always, I would venture. You know people who have incensed or irritated about some social injustice and have acted to right the wrong. Through the ages, people have used angering to fight prejudice, social wrongs, and injustices. However, angering parents have also abused children. Angering spouses have destroyed marriage relationships. Angering employees and management have demolished businesses and livelihoods.

So, to answer the question "Is angering good or bad?" one must ask another set of questions such as: Will angering help me get what I really want? Will angering in fact make my life more satisfying? Will angering strengthen or destroy the relationships that are important to me.

In each situation where the question "Is angering good or bad?" occurs, you are the person who must choose an answer to the question.

CHAPTER II
Managing Your Own Anger

I am specifically writing this portion for you. You are the person who is responsible for managing your anger in the Real World, in your family, at work and out in the community. As I am writing directly to you, I will personalize this section by using the second person pronoun, "you."

You understand that managing your anger is an important human relations skill because you recognize that angering damages and sometimes destroys relationships that are important to you. Angering can stand between you and your family members, colleagues and friends. Therefore you have caught on to the truth that keeping your angering under control is important.

But at times controlling angering is difficult to achieve. However, you are already ahead in the anger management game because you know why you anger. You know that after the first, unexpected burst of Flash Anger, you are choosing to anger because it seems to be the best way you know to make your real world more satisfying and to meet your needs in your current situation. You are probably angering to get someone's attention, or to control an individual or a situation, or as a means of avoiding acceptance of your own responsibility about something or someone.

But your angering is not working very well for you. Perhaps the angering results in your feeling more disconnected from people who are important to you. Also, people may begin to write you off when they experience your angering behavior: "Oh, he's just blowing off steam again. Ignore him and he'll soon get over it." People may resist being controlled by your angering and they may begin arguing or actually fighting with you. In any case, the angering you are choosing is simply not working. The angering is not getting you where you want to go. Your angering is not resulting in your life becoming more satisfying.

But all is not lost. You know that anger is a choice. And if angering is not getting you what you want and where you want to go, you can change your total behavior (especially your thinking and doing), stop angering and look for other behaviors that may work better. This process might not be easy. Remember that angering is an ancient behavior and has worked well for you in the past. But just right now, the angering is not doing the job and you want to make some changes.

The First Step to Manage Your Anger: Check Your Attitude.

1. First, you must acknowledge the fact that you are angering. Some people find it difficult to recognize when they anger. I have seen professional colleagues, parents, children, husbands and wives, employees and supervisors who just miss the fact they are actively choosing to anger. In order to manage your angering, it will be helpful if you conduct a "Personal Attitude Check."

When you feel either a strong physical or emotional "disease" ask yourself: "What is going on here? What are my emotions telling me? What is my body making known to me? Am I tightening and tensing my muscles? Am I changing the rate of my breathing? Am I building up emotional pressure so that I might explode? Do I feel irritated or upset about someone or something? What am I doing or saying? Am I raising my voice? Am I making a fist as I talk? Am I speaking in a way to put down or "to get the better of" the other person? Am I acting like I am in a struggle and trying to defeat the other person?

Do attitude checks while driving. How do you know when you are road raging? Possibly you give a non-verbal sign, drive recklessly or swear out loud at the other driver.

How do you know when you are angering in your home? Do you let tensions build up and then explode over something insignificant that you blow up beyond all proportions?

At work do you anger by planning "get backs"? Do you look for opportunities to talk down or denigrate a co-worker or supervisor?

Think about this for several moments and ask yourself: "How do I know when I am angering? How do I express my angering thoughts, feelings and actions?

2. Regardless of how difficult it may seem, acknowledge that angering is your choice and that no one can make you angry. Quietly chant one of these mantras to yourself: "I am choosing to anger and my angering is not

getting me where I want to be. I can change my behavior if I want." "I am in control of my behavior. I am not controlled by any person, place, thing, or system of belief that is outside me."

3. Acknowledge responsibility for the angering behavior you are choosing. Keep focused by reminding yourself: "I cannot blame my angering on anyone else. No one can push my buttons. I am not an elevator therefore, I do not have buttons; I am a person." This notion of being responsible for owning your own angering behavior is difficult for some to accept. After all, many have been using angering as an escape from facing up to personal responsibility for much of their lives. How many times have you heard statements like these: "You make me so mad when you don't get your work done on time." "When I look into your sloppy bedroom I get so mad." "When you just sit around in the evening and watch television and drink your beer, you make me so mad." REPEAT AFTER ME: "I am responsible for my behaviors; nothing or no one can make me mad. I am responsible for my own angering behaviors."

The Second Step to Managing Your Anger: Change Your Total Behavior

1. Changing your actions is a powerful and effective key to manage your angering. In order to change your angering behaviors, it is sometimes helpful to talk to yourself. Your self-talk could go something like this: "This angering just isn't working; things aren't getting any better. Am I getting closer to or further away from others? I think I'm further disconnecting myself from the very people I

want to be close to me. What am I really trying to achieve by my angering? What can I do differently to get more of what I want but without using angering?" After this self-talk get busy and identify what behavioral changes you can make and DO them.

Think for a moment about that road rage situation where the other driver pulls in front of you, cuts you off and then reduces his speed. You very well may experience Flash Anger. But you want to be a person who manages his angering; so what can you do when you recognize your flash anger? You could give a nasty hand signal, drive like a maniac yourself and endanger a dozen lives on the highway—including your own. Is that what you really want? "Heavens no," you say, "I want to get home safely and I don't want to hurt anyone. I don't actually care what that fool does. Therefore, I'm choosing to slow down for safety's sake and because I don't want to get hurt." And then you take more effective control of your behavior, drive sensibly and let the other driver go his way. You changed your angering behavior because by angering you were jeopardizing your survival need. You chose to satisfy your need for survival rather than engaging in dangerous behavior in an attempt to fulfill your need for personal power. You found life more satisfying by choosing to "let it be" and allow the other motorist to go on his way.

Consider the case of the parent who is fed up with his sixth grader's failure to complete homework assignments. The parent decides to force the issue and tries to control the child's behavior through powerful angering. The parent might say something like this: "Look, I'm sick and tired of your fooling around with that homework night after night. You're just upsetting everyone with your foolishness. Now either you do your homework or you'll wish you had. How would you like to be grounded for the next six weeks? I mean dumber kids than you can get their homework done. What's the matter with you? Do you want to grow up lazy and irresponsible? Now get in there and get to work or else!!"

What do you think the result of this parent's angering will be? I believe the parent/child relationship will be damaged and the two further disconnected from each other. And odds are that the homework will not be completed satisfactorily. The homework may or may not be completed on time, but I wonder how much thought and work will actually go into it. In my opinion, the parent's angering behavior stands an excellent chance of not working.

What behavioral changes could the parent make rather than anger at the child? The parent could listen and get the child's side of the problem; and then together they could work out a plan for both persons' needs to be satisfied. If grounding is imposed, the parent might choose to give the child an opportunity to earn a reduction or even an end to the punishment; the child could develop an acceptable plan in which he shows the parent how he will complete his homework assignments on time. The parent could choose to talk more decently to the child. The parent could spend time each night with the child and help the child to get the homework done. Or the parent could decide not to talk to the child about homework again because in fact, homework is the student's problem and not the parent's problem.

Review the following statement and then take the appropriate steps in your life: "Changing your actions is a powerful and effective key to manage your angering."

2. Modify your thinking behavior. You can actually reduce your angering by changing the thoughts in your brain. I have three suggestions for you to ponder.

First, as we noted earlier, coercion or trying to make someone do something that he doesn't want to do will usually result in angering. This also holds true for when you coerce yourself, that is, when you think you should do something you don't want to do. To eliminate this "self-coercing" behavior I suggest that you stop using the words "Should" "Ought" "Must" and "Have to" in your self-talk. You cause your own anger when you tell yourself that you "have" to do something that you do not want to do. In reality you are not giving yourself a choice. You are "demanding" something of yourself that you do not want to do.

Think about that for a moment: How many "Haves" "Oughts" "Musts" or "Shoulds" do you impose on yourself? "I *have* to take the kids to their soccer game but I don't want to; I would rather get my house work done." "I *should* make my spouse happy." "I *ought* to be a good employee and take this work home to complete.

In reality, you don't want to do any of these things, but you think you *HAVE* to do all of them. And the result is that you feel yourself tensing, getting short and snappy with people. You are angering.

Give yourself a break and quit the self-coercion. Change your thinking. How? By changing all those thinking demands to the word "PREFER" and adding "…but if I don't the world will not come to an end." For an example: "I would prefer to take the kids to their soccer game, but if I don't take them the world won't come to an end. They'll find rides with their friends." Or, "I would prefer to make my spouse a happy person, but if my mate chooses to sad the world will not come to an end." Or, "I prefer to be a good employee, but the world will not come to an end if I don't take this work home with me tonight." Thinking thoughts that essentially coerce you to act in ways that you do not want to act will result in angering.

A second suggestion has to do with your use of the word "Can't." "I would like us to take a family trip this summer, but we can't because we don't have enough money." "I want to be happy at work, but I can't because my co-workers are always interrupting me and asking me how to do their jobs." "I can't get good grades with all those preps sucking-up to the teachers." Remember that when your own thoughts prevent you from getting your needs met, you will choose angering behavior.

Instead of dwelling on what you CAN'T do, try identifying what you CAN do, and make the appropriate choices to get as much satisfaction in your life as is possible. Perhaps your family is not in the financial position to take an extended trip this summer, but what can you do? You and all your family members have needs for fun and doing things together. What can you do to meet these needs? Perhaps you could take a few day trips to near-by interesting places. Or would picnics to the mountains or the beach be satisfying? What can family members do around that house that would be fun....perhaps something different than you have done before? What CAN you do? Discovering things you can do together is the key to managing your anger.

Consider the work situation where you are headaching. What can you do differently to gain more satisfaction from your work: Could you choose to limit the time you have available for your colleagues' questions? Could you choose to let them know when it is not convenient for you to take time away from your job? What else could you do? Do not hold yourself captive of the word "Can't."

Blaming the "preps" or anyone else is no excuse for the grades you earn in school. Do you want better grades? If so, you have a hundred things you can do: You can study for tests and hand in completed homework assignments; you can ask the teacher for help; you could go to a guidance counselor and discuss your issues with her. You can join a study group. Angering and complaining about what you can't do is not a very good excuse for washingout in life.

A third suggestion relates to the pictures that you have placed in your Quality World. You will recall from our earlier discussions that we all put pictures in our Quality Worlds about how we would like things to be in the real world. Sometimes there is a conflict between the Quality World pictures of what you want and what is going on in your real world; and we have seen that you may choose angering to cope with this conflict between what you want and what you are getting.

One way to manage your angering is to change what is going on in the real world. However, often you do not have control of what is going on in the real world. But you do have control over what you put into and take out of your Quality World. Instead of trying to change the real world, you may want to examine the pictures in your Quality World and remove some pictures that are not working and add other pictures to reduce the Quality/Real World Conflict and to make your life more satisfying.

Think about that notion of changing the pictures that are in your Quality World. Suppose you picture yourself as a premiere athlete, one who is able to overcome all on the playing field. But today your team lost the game and you played poorly; the other team showed you "who was boss." There is a difference between the pictures in your Quality World and what is happening in your real world; and you are angering...at yourself, the referee and your teammates. However, you are in charge of yourself and you want to manage and control your anger. You cannot change the real world; the game has already been lost. But in order to manage your anger you could perhaps consider changing some pictures in your Quality World. How would this change work? You may readjust your picture of yourself as the athlete who can conquer all: "I am not the premiere athlete I thought I was, but I know I am good and I see myself working harder with my mind and my body to be better than I am today." This picture sounds good to me. What do you think?

Suppose that after ten years of marriage, your spouse leaves you. You are wounded, torn apart and FURIOUS. There is a huge mismatch between the pictures of what you want and what you are getting. What can you do in this situation? Managing the anger over the break-up of a marriage is not simple or easily remedied. The healing process will take some time; but if the spouse who was left behind is to get over the anger, one thing for sure will take place: She/he will add new pictures of need-satisfying people, places, things and systems of belief to her/his Quality World.

Consider the parent whose children are not acting in the real world the way the parent pictures them behaving in his/her Quality World. The pictures in the parent's Quality World have the children being dutiful, obedient, cleaning up any mess they make, doing the dishes every night, not arguing or fighting with one another and keeping their bedrooms in an orderly fashion. But in the real world, the children occasionally fight, keep their bedrooms messy, whine and complain, leave Coke bottles and cookie crumbs in the family room and worst of all they "talk back" to their parent. And this "talking back" and "not showing respect" is what really bothers the parent. Nowhere in the parent's Quality World is there a picture of a child talking back and showing disrespect. The children are not bad kids. They study, get good grades, have friends, enjoy helping around the house most of the time and all in all are pretty good youngsters. But every once in a while, the kids do have a complaint about what's going on in the family, and they do make their displeasure known. The parent likes the children and the children like the parent; but parental angering rears its ugly head when the parent perceives the children "talking back." The parent realizes that her relationship with the children will be hurt if she keeps angering over this problem. She wants to control herself and manage this angering. We have seen how a parent can change both behavior and thinking to manage anger. Now, what pictures can the parent add to the Quality World to cope with his angering when the children "back talk?" What about this picture? Instead of angering when the children argue and talk back, perhaps the parent could picture himself LISTENING to the children's complaints. The parent could add a picture to her Quality World in which she would not anger when the kids "back-talked;" rather, he would listen to them and try to understand the kids' points of view. I would suspect that by adding this picture to his Quality World, the parent not only would manage his angering, but she also would help the children manage their angering; as nothing intensifies the flames of angering as does fighting fire with fire. The parent's angering can only cause more problems in the parent/child relationship. Therefore, the parent is choosing responsible behavior by searching out new pictures to put in her Quality World...pictures that will reduce parent/child tensions.

My mother told me a long time ago that "To live is to adjust." And I think what she was implying is this: When pictures in your Quality World no longer meet your needs and fail to provide a satisfying life, perhaps it is time for you to add a few new pictures and weed out a few others.

You may wonder how changing actions, thoughts and pictures in your Quality World may help you to feel less distraught, less irritated and less irate. I ask you to recall the concept of Total Behavior as an integrated system and when one element of total behavior is changed, there are shifts and changes in the other elements. When you make changes in what you think or what you do, you certainly will see changes in your physiology and your emotions.

The Third Step to Managing Your Anger: A Quick Review Of Why You Continue Holding On to Angering Behavior

If by this time you are still having problems managing your angering and continue to anger, you can bet your bottom dollar angering is meeting your needs some how. In order to quickly get in control and manage your choice angering, you may want to run down this list of questions and get a better grip on the behavioral choices you are making.

1. I am choosing to anger and my angering really isn't getting me what I want in my life and in my relationships. What am I trying to achieve by my angering? What am I trying to really get by angering?

2. Am I trying to get ATTENTION? From whom do I want attention? How can I get the attention I want and not destroy the relationship? I know angering disconnects people from each other and destroys relationships?

3. Am I AVOIDING my responsibility and trying to put blame on someone else for my discomfort and pain? What can I do to take responsibility for my behavior, deeds and thoughts?

4. Who or what am I trying to CONTROL through my angering? Will this angry controlling get me what I really want? Or will controlling through my angering drive away the very people I want to have closer to me? Are my attempts to control worth the price of disconnected relationships that I will have to pay for in the long run? What can I do differently?

The Fourth Step to Managing Your Anger: A Serious Talk With Yourself

If you continue choice angering after studying and using the first three steps, now is the time to sit down and have a serious talk with yourself. Using all the information we have discussed to this point—-the issues of choice, responsibility, relationship, basic needs, total behavior and angering as an attempt to make life more satisfying, to refresh your memory—-get answers to the following questions.

1. What do I really want? What are the pictures in my Quality World that I am trying to activate in my real world? I know I have basic needs for survival, power, love and belonging, freedom and fun. Where is the conflict

between what I want and what is happening in the real world? What am I trying to achieve?

2. I recognize that I am choosing anger to get what I want. Is this angering working for me or against me? I know through angering I can sometimes manipulate others into doing what I want....at least for a while. But I also know that if I anger too regularly in my relationships, I will drive people away from me; is that what I want? Is my angering getting me closer or further away from what I really want? Is my angering working: Yes or No?

3. If your angering is working for you and if you are getting what you really want through angering, good luck. Keep on doing what you're doing. You can call me in the morning or see me at the clinic in a month or so. However, if your answer is "No. My angering is not getting me what I want." you have another question to answer: Do I want to continue being stuck in my angering, or do I want to change my behavior and find a way to meet my needs and yet not use destructive angering? Yes or No again.

4. If I want to change, what can I do differently to meet my basic needs and find a more satisfying life? I can make a plan. The plan will specify:

   a. What I will do differently (i.e. noting specific behavior and thinking changes or identifying additional need-meeting pictures to add to my Quality World)?

   b. A time line which clearly shows deadlines, benchmarks and target dates when I will make these changes.

c. Since I am in control of my behavior, I will make these changes regardless of what others do or say because I think the changes will help me find a more need-satisfying life while at the same time not endangering the relationships which I value and hold dear.

d. If this plan is unsuccessful, I will not be deterred; I will make a new plan.

Thank you for staying with me through this process. By now you know everything I know about how you can manage your anger. Nonetheless, you are in charge of the rest of the story. To paraphrase Shakesphere: "To anger or not to anger; that is the question." The answer, however dear reader, is your choice.

Chapter III
Helping the Other Person Manage His/Her Anger

In this section we will explore skills and methods you may choose to assist another person manage his/her angering behavior. You may be a parent, husband or wife, teacher, manager, counselor or friend. In any case you have chosen to help the other person reduce or eliminate angering behavior. Let me clarify at the very outset what the defining characteristic of the helping person's role is. You are acting as counselor-helper and you cannot expect the other person to deal with YOUR angering behavior. You cannot expect the angering person to counsel you. As counselor-helper, you are responsible for managing your own angering by using the skills we discussed in the previous section.

As you already know, you will be helping the other person to manage two kinds of anger: Flash Anger and Choice Anger. Flash Anger is that sudden, strong sense of displeasure that seems to "just happen" when something goes radically "wrong" in a person's life. You also know that if the other person continues angering after that first, unexpected burst of Flash Anger, he/she is choosing Choice Anger. Choice Anger is the individual's best attempts to make his/her real world more satisfying, that is, to meet his/her needs for survival, power, love and belonging, freedom and fun. Therefore, we will be discussing the two specific sets of skills to manage these distinct expressions of angering. They are: (1) skills to de-fuse the powerful explosions of Flash Anger and (2) a process through which you can aid the angering individual to move beyond Choice Anger and make behavioral choices to meet needs without angering.

But first of all, I want to explore the very important and oftentimes confusing subject of the "helper role."

A. The Role of Helper

A "helper" is one who offers aid, support, succor or whatever is necessary to assist another person to accomplish something. The anger-management helper assists the angering person to:

(1) de-fuse angering behavior and get more in control of himself,

(2) identify what she truly is trying to achieve by angering,

(3) self-evaluate the effectiveness of his angering behavior,

(4) decide whether to continue angering or not, and

(5) make decisions about what behaviors will meet her needs and heal relationships without choosing to anger.

You have already been armed with knowledge that will aid you in your helping responsibilities: You know why the other person is angering. You know he angers to meet his needs for survival, power, love and belonging, freedom and fun and to make his life more satisfying. You know she chooses anger to ask, "Help me. Pay attention to me." You know she angers as a means of avoiding doing something she doesn't want to do or is afraid to do. She chooses anger to control someone or something. Or he chooses anger to pump himself up and feel big and strong. You know that angering is a focused and purposefully chosen behavior. You know the angering person is doing the best she knows to meet her needs and achieve a more satisfying life.

As the helper, you are responsible for creating the "therapeutic environment" in which the angering person can reduce and eliminate the angering behavior. Your attitude toward the angering person is a most important factor in whether you can develop this environment and help that individual manage his angering or not. In life, it is usually "natural" for you to fight back or get safely away when you confront an angering person. Therefore, "helping" is somewhat of an unnatural behavior for if you are to really help the angering person you will face up to him and you will not fight back.

In order to create the therapeutic, helping environment, I would suggest that you calmly and honestly self-assess your attitude toward angering people and see if you can:

a. Accept the angering person for what she is—a person who is trying the best she knows how to meet her needs. He may have learned irresponsible, angering ways to meet these needs; therefore, he has some re-learning to do. And as a helper, that is what you are there for.

b. Avoid finding fault with the angering person. You may not appreciate her behavior, but faultfinding will only worsen the situation. Avoid communicating blame.... either verbally or non-verbally.

c. Avoid being judgmental. No one likes to be told that they have "missed the mark" and are therefore less than should be. If the helper communicates this attitude, she will very soon lose the job as helper. Very few of us would ever accept aid from someone who puts us down.

d. Refrain from trying to make the angering person do or think something he doesn't want to do or think. The angering person probably has a strong need for freedom, to make her own decisions. Pressuring or manipulating the angry person to do something she does not want to do is simply coercion and will quickly bring an end to the helping session. Would you accept help from someone who tries to force you to do or think something you do not want to do or think?

e. Stay out of the conflict. Do not allow yourself to become debilitated by the other's anger. Put your defensiveness and arguing aside; they will be no help here. Getting yourself heated up and counterattacking punch for punch with the angering person will only damage or destroy the helping relationship.

f. Believe that the angering person does have the right to make decisions and choices about how he meets his needs and that she does have within her the ability to make those decisions. The helper's job is to give assistance so the angering person can make life-decisions in a responsible manner, that is, through behaviors that do not hurt himself, the helper, others, damage relationships or are against the law.

g. Try to see the situation from the angering person's point of view and understand what needs she is trying to satisfy. You know that an attempt to meet basic needs is at the root of the angering. What is the angering person trying to achieve?

h. Remember that your helping job is to give aid and assist in the healing of relationships. Your job is healing, not "getting back" for wrongs or hurts that you may have suffered at the hands of the angering person. "Getting Even" is an unacceptable attitude for the helping person to embrace.

Before we consider the anger de-fusing skills, I want to offer three warnings to the potential anger-management helping person:

1. Through your words, deeds and attitude you may be able to provide the environment in which the angering person is able to find safety, reduce the heat and bring down the explosive angering energy. However, you cannot control the angering person's behavior; you cannot make the other person stop angering. He/she is responsible for making his/her behavioral choices. Actually, you must acknowledge your powerlessness to change another's angering behavior; you have control over your own angering not over another's angering.

2. Do not expect the angering person to help you manage your anger. While in the act of angering, a person does

not have the capability to help you. You are the helper, and if your angering is getting in the way, you are the one who must do something about it!!

3.   Avoid fighting fire with fire. Angering at the other person who is also angering can only result in something that is extremely ugly. If you cannot maintain a helping attitude and you feel yourself choosing to anger, get out of the helping role. Discontinue the session until you are able to maintain the responsible helping attitudes. You will be doing yourself and the other individual a large favor.

Enough!!! Now on to the actual de-fusing skills.

B.   Skills to De-fuse Flash Anger

When you come face to face with a person who is Flash Angering, what do you see? How is that person acting? He might be yelling, making threats, not thinking clearly, criticizing, blaming, unable to be logical or reasonable, raging or hostile. The angering person may even be verbally attacking you or threatening you physically.

Your job as the helper is that of assisting the angering person to reduce the heat, lower his emotional temperature and de-fuse the "anger bomb" before there is a terrible explosion. You, "The De-fuser," help the other person to get in more effective control and to think rationally rather than to explode. I am suggesting four skills to assist you.

1. Active Passive Listening: Active Passive Listening is a demanding skill. Active Passive Listening requires you to

a. Open your ears

b. Shut your mouth

c. Focus your attention on what the angering person is saying.

Active Passive Listening requires that you diligently keep focused on the other person's message that he/she is communicating through angry behaviors and words. This means that while you are listening with your ears open and your mouth shut, your mind is attentive and alert. You know the angering behavior is probably a shout for attention or an attempt to control the situation. Ask yourself: "What message is the angering person trying to have me hear? What does this person really want? What is the picture from his Quality World that is in conflict with the Real World? Which of the basic psychological needs is the person trying to meet through angering?"

Active Passive Listening sounds like an easy skill to do. It isn't. All too often instead of Active Passive Listening the "de-fusing" person focuses his/her mind on making a defensive, justifying response to the angering person. Try to calm the situation by not feeding your own ideas and issues into the exchange at this time. Remember, your job in working with the person who is Flash Angering is to de-fuse the bomb not to stir up additional excitement. Negotiation, where you can discuss your concerns, will come later when the angering person has cooled down and is able to think rationally.

2. Acknowledgement: Through the acknowledging response you are communicating this message, "Yes, I hear you. Please continue." An acknowledging response may be as simple as "Wow," "Un-huh," or "And then

what?" You may want to acknowledge the frustration or hurt that you hear the angering person expressing by saying something like: "Golly, it sounds like you had a miserable day. No wonder you are upsetting and irritating." Or, "Yep, I can see what's firing you up." Non-verbally communicate your acknowledgement by nodding your head. A non-blameful, non-critical acknowledgement of the other's angering may help to de-fuse the high explosive fury of Flash Angering.

3. Agreeing with Two-Percent of the Truth: This skill may sound naïve and oversimplified. And it is true that you will very quickly understand the concept. But much practice, discipline and self-restraint are necessary if you want to make use of effective agreeing statements. Nevertheless the work is well worth the effort as agreeing is one of the most effective skills you can have in your de-fusing arsenal.

To understand the agreeing statement consider this question: How is one usually inclined to respond to a person who is Flash Angering? If left to our natural tendencies, I believe most of us will choose a defensive counterattack by identifying the 98% of what the angering person is saying with which we DISAGREE and then firing back our self-justifications, arguments and explanations of why we disagree with that 98%. This response usually has negative results causing the Flash Angering fire to blaze hotter while absolutely no de-fusing takes place; the situation deteriorates.

To reduce the high emotional energy of Flash Angering, you might want to consider replying with the opposite response. Instead of looking for the 98% of what you disagree with, search out the 2% of what the person is saying that you can actually AGREE with. After all, you have been actively passive listening to the person's flash angering. You have paid attention to the messages that the angering person is sending. There must be at least 2% of what he said with which you could agree either in fact or in principle. After you have identified the 2% with which you are able to agree, formulate and offer an "agreeing statement". An agreeing statement is in two parts:

a. "You're right...

b. Then add the 2% of truth."

Let's practice making "agreeing statements." Suppose a teenage daughter or son says to you:

"You're always on my case. I can't do anything without having you get in my face. I can't do anything right according to you. Sometimes I feel like just leaving here and going somewhere else so I wouldn't have to put up with your putting me down."

I imagine you won't have any trouble finding the 98% of the message with which you disagree. You are not in her face all the time. You are not always criticizing her. You do think that he can do lots of things and do them well. And you know he can't leave home and live elsewhere; that just will not work.

But what could you agree with? Yes, I do get in her face from time to time. I do point out his errors and shortcomings. I bet that sometimes he does feel like getting away for a break.

So, let's put together a possible agreeing statement that you, the helper, might say to the angering person:

"You're right. I do get on your case."

Or, "You're right. I do have a lot to say sometimes."

Or, "You're right. Sometimes I do tend to be critical."

An agreeing statement seems so simple to formulate as you calmly read this material. Making agreeing statements is much more difficult and demanding when a student, spouse, child, employee, customer or neighbor is face to face with you, muscles tensing and telling you in an emotional, harsh voice how you have done wrong or failed. Faced with this situation if we responded "naturally" most of us would be sorely tempted to return the anger, argue or defend ourselves. The effective anger-management helper will resist that temptation.

Let's take another example. Your spouse is upsetting and is letting you know about it.

"Remember two weeks ago I asked you to fix that problem. We discussed it and you agreed to repair it. Every day you promise to fix it; but everything and everyone else comes first. You don't pay attention to what I want. You're always busy being such a good person to your mother and to other people that you don't have any time left over for me. You're not concerned about what I need. You don't care about me."

Can you make an agreeing statement that will help calm down the situation with your spouse? Of course, you can pick out the statements with which you could argue. But you know that arguing or defending yourself will not de-fuse the situation. What is 2% of the truth with which you can honestly agree? And can you make an agreeing statement?

How about:

> "You're right. I don't pay enough attention to your concerns."

> "You're right. I could more effectively show that I care about you."

> "You're right. Sometimes I do put what you want on the back burner."

You may want to keep this formula for creating an effective agreeing statement in mind:

> "You're right + 2% of truth with which you could agree." PERIOD!

Stop right there at the end of the agreeing statement and say no more. Do not ruin a perfectly good agreeing statement by adding a "but" and going on to argue or tell the angering person where he/she is wrong or show him/her how s/he is making a mountain out of a mole hill. To offer an effective agreeing statement, you will not yield to the temptation of adding your own ideas, thoughts and feelings. Presenting your own issues while the other person is Flash Angering will only serve to raise the angering person's emotional energy which is counterproductive to your job of helping the person to de-fuse.

4. Inviting Criticism: As criticism and blame tend to heighten the emotional energy of Flash Angering, frequently the opposite response will decrease the intensity

of the anger and increase the likelihood of de-fusing. You may even find that "Inviting Criticism" is a powerful defusing tool that often is the turning point between Flash Angering and finding a solution for the conflict. The Inviting Criticism response is usually in the form of a non-defensive question in which the helper simply invites the angering person to voice his/her criticism of the helper.

"How did I offend you?" asks the helper.

"What did I do wrong?" asks the helper.

"What would you rather have me do?" asks the helper.

"What could I do differently next time?" asks the helper.

"What would you like to see happen?" asks the helper.

As with any of the de-fusing skills, the helper will be wise to resist the temptation to become defensive and argue back when the Flash Angering person accepts the offer to criticize.

When Your De-fusing Interventions Are Not Getting The Results You Want, Consider These Notions.

The following is a list of possible correctives that you may use to sharpen and strengthen your de-fusing skills.

1. Don't expect too much too soon. Prepare yourself to use enough skillful responses to thoroughly de-fuse the situation. I have seen only a few flash angering people who could keep angering after being confronted with eight or nine effective de-fusing responses. Do not be in a rush to move on to a solution while the other person continues to anger. Remember, while he is flash angering, the other

person does not have the cognitive ability to think logically and reasonably.

2. Traditional "Active Listening" is not very effective with some people when they are Flash Angering. Active Listening sometimes communicates the message: "I, the helper, am well. You, the angering person, are sick, in need or somehow inferior to me." Try Active Passive Listening first.

3. You are the helper; do not criticize or blame the angering person. Asking the angering person to "justify" or "explain" his position is very often understood as criticism. Be careful about the questions you ask. Avoid the question "Why" at all costs during the time you are trying to help the angering person de-fuse her Flash Anger.

4. Are you non-verbally canceling what you are verbally communicating? A frown or shaking your head can effectively say "No" even though your words are saying "Yes." Be careful of what your non-verbal actions are communicating.

5. Logic and reason simply are not effective with the angering person. Your logical, reasonable and rational suggestions will only sound like criticism or blame to the one who is Flash Angering.

6. Resist getting into the fray. Avoid arguing, answering back defensively or trying to have the angering person understand your point of view. Wait until the Flash Angering has been de-fused and the other person is more ready to hear your side of the issue.

7. Hold back on expressing your own ideas. Recall that your ideas and suggestions, which are logical and reasonable to you, only sound like criticism and blame to the person who is angering.

8. One of the biggest errors a helper can make is this: Responding to Flash Angering with an effective de-fusing statement and ruining it all by not stopping right there. "You're right. I should listen more; BUT you don't listen very well yourself." As you can imagine the helper has just lost all credibility.

9. Be honest with yourself and the angering person. Do not pretend to agree with the other person if you cannot honestly find a percentage of truth in the angry person's statements. Do not degrade the angering person by making a condescending, untruthful agreeing statement.

C.   Skills to Manage Choice Anger

In this section, we will consider the interventions you can make to help the angering person move beyond Choice Angering. You will recall that Choice Angering is the individual's attempt to make his/her real world more satisfying, that is, to fulfill his/her needs for survival, power, love and belonging, freedom and fun; and he chooses angering behavior to meet these needs. Choice Angering may be the behavior that quickly follows on the heels of Flash Angering. Or Choice Angering may be chosen without the person first Flash Angering; Choice Angering may, so to speak, stand alone without the explosions of Flash Angering. How do you know when a person is choosing angering? A person usually sends one of these three signals when angering:

(1) She tells you directly: "I'm really burned up the way Sally is treating me and the others on our team. I'm really angry."

(2) He sends a strong expression of a negative emotion: "That blasted history teacher failed me. I hate that place. School is just stupid. I don't know why I have to go there; I never learn anything anyhow."

(3) A person may express angering silently or non-verbally. A scowl may send the "I'm angry." message. Sometimes pouting and withdrawal are signs of angering: "Nothing's wrong. I just don't have anything to say right now, and if I did say something, you more than likely wouldn't want to hear it anyhow."

The helper's objective is to (1) provide the therapeutic environment and (2) aid the person to move beyond angering and to meet his/her needs for survival, power, love and belonging, freedom and fun without choosing angering behavior.

In this section we will discuss two types of situations of moving beyond angering. The first is where you, the helper, are assisting the angering person to cope with a problem or conflict that does not involve you personally. You are not an object of or directly related to the angering person's conflict. In this situation, the person is angering to cope with a situation involving something or someone beyond you such as school, friends, work, or whatever.

The second case is where you, the helper, are directly involved in the person's anger: He is mad at you for something you have done or said. For an example, if you are a parent, the child may be angering about a decision you made. If you are a teacher, the student may be angering over a grade or discipline.

If you are a supervisor, the employee may be upsetting over the work schedule you posted. If you are a merchant, the customer may be angrily complaining about a purchase that has gone wrong or unsatisfactory.

As you can imagine each situation, where you are and where you are not an object of the angering person's ire, requires its own specific set of skills.

Let us first consider the case where you, the helper, are not directly involved with the other person's angering. Here your goal is to provide the therapeutic environment where the angering person can fully explore his situation, make logical/rational decisions and develop a plan to achieve a more satisfying life without choosing angering. I am suggesting the following as a guide for you to point out the way for the other person as he moves toward a satisfying life with much less angering.

1. Developing the therapeutic environment, the arena in which your helping is acknowledged and accepted, is a most important first step. You may wish to review the material on developing the therapeutic environment, which I included in the section on the role of the helper earlier in this chapter. If the angering person does not perceive you as a helper, if you are not a person who is in her Quality World as someone she can trust, there is not much you can do to help her manage her anger. The helper's attitude and actions must communicate this message: "I'm here to help you get as much of what you want as is humanly possible as long as what you want is not illegal, or not going to hurt yourself or someone else." I cannot overstate the importance of the helper's avoiding communicating messages, which

convey blame, criticism and coercion. Would you accept help from a person who criticizes you or blames you or tries to make you do something you don't want to do? The helper can only expect to experience an explosion of Flash Anger if he/she employs any of these dangerous interventions.

2. Help the angering person to identify and state what he is trying to achieve through angering. You know she is choosing angering behavior to somehow make her world more satisfying: What does she want? Here the helper might ask questions like: "How would you like your life to be?" "What are you trying to achieve through your angering?" "What's your picture of the way you would like the situation to be?" "In your opinion, how do you see things if they were shaped up the way you wanted?" "What would you like to see happen?" "How would you like to see things changed?" I am suggesting that you use visual terms in your interventions, as the helper's job here is to assist the angering person to identify and focus the pictures in her Quality World. What are the pictures in her Quality World that she would like to see alive and operating in her Real World?

3. After the angering person has identified what she really is trying to achieve by angering, the helper must ask a most important question. The self-evaluation question will help to bring the results of angering behavior into focus: "Is your angering really getting you where you want to go? Will your angering help you get what you want? Is your angering working for you?" The helper holds out until the angering person makes either a "Yes"

or "No" answer. The angering person is the only person who can provide an answer to this question. If the helper makes the evaluation ("Well, I really don't think that your angering will get you where you want to go.") the angering person will only perceive this intervention as criticism, blame or a veiled manipulation to do something she doesn't want to do. The helper's evaluation will certainly result in defensiveness and a re-kindled blaze of Flash Angering. On the other hand, if the helper assists the angering person to make a self-evaluation, the process of moving beyond anger will be greatly enhanced. If the angering person answers "Yes, my angering is getting me what I want." the helper may have to be satisfied with letting the matter drop for now and wait for a time when the other person signals that she is ready to address her angering. If the answer to the self-evaluation question is "No. My angering is not getting me what I want." we are ready to move the counseling process on to the next stage.

4. At this point, it would be most proper for the helper to ask a question that offers the angering person a choice: "OK. So your anger isn't working. Now what do you want to do? Do you want to keep on angering and getting the same results? Or do you want to explore some alternatives through which you can get more of what you want?" This seems like a simple question, but it lays the foundation for establishing a realistic, responsible plan to move beyond angering.

5. Establishing a plan of action will enable the other person to take charge of his/her life and make choices to

achieve a more satisfying life without angering. A plan answers three questions:

a. Who?

b. Is to do what?

c. By when?

Exactly who (The angering person? The helper? Some other person?) is going to do precisely what? The best plans state what actions will be carried out in specific, measurable terms that are concretely stated. The more specifically the plan is spelled out, the more likely it is that the desired results will be accomplished, that is, for the angering person to achieve a more satisfying life with less angering. If the student devises a plan where he "tries" to get his homework done every night, I would predict a low possibility for success. Avoid "waffling words" like "try" or "attempt." Together, clearly spell out what the angering person will do to gain a more satisfying life. And state when these actions will take place. The more specific you can make the plan, the more chance the angering person has to move beyond anger. Also, do not trust that the plan will be remembered even if the angering person has the best intentions. Write the plan and ask the angering person to sign the plan. And you, the helper, will also sign the plan. Set a time when you and the angering person will review the plan's results. If the results have not been satisfactory, a new plan can be created. "If at first you don't succeed, try again."

Now let us consider the situation where you, the helper, are directly involved in the other person's angering. The angering person is pointing his ire, his outrage, at you! You are part of the angering person's problem! However, you also have chosen to be the helper and to be an active agent in developing the solution. To tell you the truth, this position of being both the helper and the object of anger will tax your skills and psychological resources. But if you observe the following suggestions, I am sure, with practice, you will be able to manage this situation expertly.

Your goal as helper is to (1) help the angering person stay at a defused level and (2) provide the necessary aid so that the angering person and you are able to work out an acceptable, responsible and realistic resolution of the conflict. The target is for you both to get your needs satisfied as much as possible without harming each other or any other person through behaviors that are not against the law. You will seek to achieve this solution through a process that runs a low risk of endangering the relationship between you and the angering person.

Step 1. Maintain the therapeutic, helping environment even though the other person is angering directly at you. Remember that you are in control of your own behavior; the angering person cannot "push your button" or "make" you angry. Arguing back, becoming defensive, counter-punching or meeting fire with fire will only destroy your opportunity to help develop a solution to the problem. During the discussion if you hear the angering person's emotional energy getting "hotter", then you know what to do: Step in with defusing skills. If the angering person's emotional energy goes up, help him/her bring it down by inviting criticism or sending an agreeing statement. Defusing skills are as important in this circumstance as they are in de-fusing Flash Angering.

Summary of Step 1: Keep your angering in check and remain cool. Meeting anger with anger will cause a destructive explosion.

Step 2. After the angering person's ire has been de-fused and her emotional energy is lowered, she is now more ready to think logically and realistically and to enter into the problem solving process. When you sense this readiness, ask the angering person to commit to joining with you and creating a solution that meets her needs and your needs. Such a request might sound something like this: "Look. I think that if we work together we can figure this problem out. I want to find a solution that we both can live with. Will you work with me to develop a plan that is effective?" Do be patient; do not push, manipulate or coerce for an immediate commitment from the angering person. If he seems hesitant to work with you, listen and understand the angry person's reservations and doubts. Coercing or manipulating the angry person into a commitment, which he really does not want, is unacceptable. If the helper uses manipulation or coercion at this early stage of finding a solution, the helping environment and the helper's credibility are severely weakened.

Summary of Step 2: Try to get a commitment to work together to find a solution and "Working together to find a solution" does not mean, "We're going to do it my way."

Step 3. Ask the angering person: "Where is the problem? What are our differences? What's going wrong?" And then get ready to listen and de-fuse without criticism, blame or self-justification. After the angering person has fully communicated his/her concerns, you can share your perceptions of the problem. Use statements that do not suggest blame or criticism: Take ownership of your problems by sending I-Messages not You-Messages. I-Messages begin with the pronoun "I" and tend to be less blameful or critical than statements that begin with the pronoun "You." Compare the following two messages. Which one sounds friendlier to you—the "I-Message" or the "You-Message"? "You always keep your room so messy and cluttered. You should be more respectful of your property." Or "I would really appreciate it if you kept your room more tidy." Is there any contest?

Summary of Step 3: The aim is to clarify the problem not to assign blame or guilt.

Step 4. After clearly spelling out the problem/conflict, ask the angering person: "We've identified the problem. Now what do you see as our strengths? What do we have going for us?" This is the time to identify the strengths in the relationship as you and the angry person see them. The strengths, the positives, in the relationship are too often over-looked or ignored. The notion here is to use the strengths that you identify to build a solid solution. "Building a Solution on Strengths" is much sounder than building a solution merely to "solve the problem." Asking the angering person to help you identify strengths in the relationship will go a long way toward setting a positive tone which will strengthen the relationship and aid in solution finding. S/he may well be surprised at your request and falter at first. However, stay with it.

Summary of Step 4: Model strength identification behaviors and help the angering person to recognize personal and relationship strengths that are the building blocks of a responsible, realistic solution.

Step 5. Ask the angering person: "What can each of us do to make the situation more the way we want it to be?" What actions can each individual, the helper as well as the angering person, choose to make the situation more satisfying and fulfilling? Both persons have pictures in their Quality Worlds of how their needs for survival, power, love and belonging, freedom and fun can be met. Which of these pictures can be placed in the real world without causing conflicts? What behaviors can each person choose to make the situation more satisfying—regardless of the choices that the other person makes? This is not a case where "I will do this only if you will do that." Each person will choose his/her actions to make the situation better and be responsible for these choices.

Summary of Step 5: What can we both do to make this situation more satisfying for both of us?

Step 6. Commit the plan to paper. Write who is going to do what and by when? Then both persons—the helper and the angering person—will sign the written plan. Mutually decide when both the angering person and the helper will together review the plan. Agree to no unilateral modifications of the plan. After all this has been completed, post the plan on the fridge and put it into action. Therapy is begun in any situation when the person who is having the problem takes the first steps to do something about making his life more satisfying; the same holds true in resolving problem angering. Review the plan at the agreed-upon time. And if it is not working, change the plan so that the actions will get both people, angering and helping, where they want to go.

Summary of Step 6: Doing is the key to healing the cancerous blister of angering.

"Just don't stand there: Do something."

Now you possess the knowledge to de-fuse and help the other person move beyond angering. This knowledge, in and of itself, accomplishes very little. To have this knowledge achieve the desired results, you must put it into practice:

CHAPTER IV
Obstacles to Effective Anger Management

"There is always something to upset the most careful of human plans."

C.E.Confer

If you are not getting the results you wish from your anger managing efforts, I suggest that you review the following obstacles to effective anger management. Ask yourself the self-evaluating question: "Am I setting up any of these obstacles when I am trying to help?" If you find that you are, you may very well want to change your interventions. Also, avoiding the damaging interventions in your every day involvement with others will help prevent the development of angering in your personal relationships.

1. You have chosen to be an anger manager. At all times throughout the anger management process it is important to maintain the therapeutic environment. You are the counselor. Do not expect that the angering child, spouse, employee, neighbor or student will be concerned with your needs while they are angering. You are meeting your

needs through helping and restoring the relationship to health. Do not expect the angering person to appreciate your efforts.

2. Trying to work out a solution while the other person is hotly angering is fruitless. First put out the fire and then negotiate a solution.

3. Try to keep in mind that angering has worked for the other person. By angering she has gained much attention, avoided taking responsibility for his behaviors and controlled situations and people. Therefore, expecting an immediate response to abandon angering behaviors may be unrealistic. New behaviors that move beyond angering will take time to perfect. Practice patience. To help prevent angering in your home, school, office or neighborhood, please keep in mind the notion that people behave in order to create a satisfying life, that is, to meet their basic physical and psychological needs. In healthy relationships, people help others to satisfy those needs in ways that do not harm people or personal relationships and that are not against the law. As a helper, you can prevent or reduce the amount of angering in your home, school, office or community by helping others meet their needs...without the necessity of resorting to anger.

4. Consider if you are using any of the "Dangerous Six" in your relationships with others. Avoiding these interventions in your personal relationships will go a long way toward preventing outbursts of Flash Anger. Any use of these roadblocks with angering persons will result in continued and increased angering.

a Angering—If you fight back by meeting angering with angering, fighting fire with fire, you can expect anger management failure and damaged relationships.

b Arguing—Arguing with the angering person gets you deeper into the fray.

c Blame—Blame is finding fault with, censuring or expressing disapproval of the other person's errors or mistakes. When you lay blame on a person she perceives that in your eyes she is WRONG. Few of us will accept help from people who judge that we are wrong.

d Criticism—Criticism is a severe unfavorable judgment as to the merits of a person, thing or belief. When you criticize, you are telling a person he is dumb, stupid, ignorant, insensitive or lazy and that he is bad. Criticism is an easy way to destroy any personal relationship. And remember this: No matter what your parents said, there is no such thing as constructive criticism. Constructive and criticism are contradictory terms. If I criticize you, even with the best of intentions, I am telling you that you are BAD.

e Coercion—Coercion is an attempt to force or manipulate someone to do something he doesn't want to do. Coercion not only destroys the therapeutic-helping environment, it murders family and personal relationships. I suspect that coercion is the single most effective destroyer of personal relationships. Avoid pressuring people into places they do not want to be.

f. Defensiveness—When you are trying to nourish the helping environment, defensiveness causes the plant to wither away and die. Whether you mean it or not, defensiveness implies the message, "I'm right. You're wrong. Listen to me and get it right." This is not the message that engenders trust in either personal relationships or your anger managing abilities and skills.

5. Angering people have used angering behavior to successfully avoid taking responsibility for their actions. Those who anger sometimes try to justify their actions by telling you about their difficulties in childhood, how parents mistreated them, or how people have misused and abused them or treated them poorly. And much of this data is true, factual. However, let us not lose sight of this truth: Angering is causing them problems with their relationships in the here and now; angering is standing in the way of obtaining a satisfying life. If the helper accepts these excuses and falls into the trap of the angering person's victimization, how can the angering person be helped to move beyond anger? If the angering person holds on to wrath, how can a satisfying life be found, that is, a life where relationships are not destroyed and people are not driven further away? Do not accept the angering person's attempts to avoid responsibility for behaviors through victim-ing.

6. Bribing the angering person with rewards, praise, prizes or other manipulative carrots will not be effective. "If you do this, then you can have that." is a bribe and manipulation. The angering person will quickly see through your ploy to buy him off and get him to do something he really doesn't want to do. You may get a

quick, short-lived positive result, as the angering person wants the "that"; but she is not interested in the slightest with doing the "this" for any length of time after the reward is withdrawn.

7. Some counselors and therapists insist that the angering person must gain "insight" and understand "why" he is angering. You know why she is angering: Angering is the best behavior she knows to meet her needs for survival, power, love and belonging, freedom and fun. Spending time digging around in the other person's past is largely wasted time. Our goal in managing angering is to help the angering person to live in the NOW and make choices that will lead to a more satisfying life now and in the future. The past is dead and gone. The future lies ahead. What can the angering person do NOW to point his life in the direction that holds the promise of need-meeting satisfactions?

8. You do not control the other's behavior. You cannot make the other person either mad or happy. The other person chooses his/her behavior. If the angering person continues to choose anger to meet his/her needs for attention, avoidance or control s/he must be allowed to live with the consequences of that behavior. Do your best to de-fuse and help the other to move beyond anger: That is your responsibility as "helper." The angering person makes his/her behavioral choices and must live with the results.

ENDPIECE

Through your study of this material, I trust you have gained some understanding of the dynamics of angry behavior. I hope you are encouraged to practice skills that manage both your own anger and the anger of another person. I am confident that you have generated some ideas about how to prevent destructive anger from damaging your personal and professional relationships. Best wishes to you as you move on from here. The work of managing anger is difficult and demanding. But the rewards when you are successful are most gratifying.

Appendix A
An Example of a Parent Managing a Young Teen's Angering.

T=Teen's comments
P=Parent's intervention

P1   Going out? Be home at 11:00. OK?

T1   11:00? You must be kidding. No one comes home at 11:00 anymore.

P2   I thought we had agreed on 11:00 for Friday nights because you have soccer practice early Saturday.

T2   Yeah. Agreement. If that's what you call it. I call it more like living in a prison camp. You're always on my case. Do this. Do that. Always bringing up that agreement stuff. Why don't you just take care of yourself and I'll take care of myself?

P3   Yes. You're right. I am on your case sometimes.

T3   I'd say more than sometimes. You're on my case about what time I come home, my friends and my grades. You always gripe about my grades.

P4   You're right. I am concerned about your grades.

T4 Well, why don't you spend some of your time worrying about Mark? Wow! Just because he's seventeen you let him do everything he wants. Why aren't you on his case, too? Just because he's three years older than I am he can do anything.

P5 Right. Mark is seventeen. You're right.

T5 He's so much of a jerk. You don't know half the stuff he does. But I do. If you knew as much as I do about what Mark does you would be on his case, too.

P6 You're right, Kevin, I don't know everything that Mark does.

T6 Well, I'm just getting tired of perfect Mark being allowed to do whatever he wants and you and Mom being on my case all the time.

P7 Well, Kevin, how would you like it to be? What changes would you make around here?

T7 Everyone would get off my back.

P8 OK, what would be different if we, as you say, got off your back?

T8 I don't know exactly. I could do more of what I want.

P9 Your mother and I want you to get as much of what you want as is possible. What would you change in order to get more of what you want?

T9 I'd stay out all night and come in when I want to.

P10 Do you really think that will fly here in this household?

T10 Nah. You would never allow that I guess.

P11 Yep, you're right. Staying out all night won't fly. So what else would you change?

T11 I don't know. But I hate coming in at 11:00 when everyone else stays until 11:30.

P12 So we're talking about a half an hour here?

T12 I know it seems small potatoes to you. But it's important to me.

P13 OK. It's important. I have a concern because when you come home even at eleven o'clock, you don't go to bed until much later. And then I have a dickens of a time getting you up for soccer practice at nine in the morning. You see my point?

T13 Yeah.

P14 So what do you think we could do to not have you feel odd man out at the teen center and yet meet my needs not to have a complete furor in the morning before you go to soccer.

T14 But I like to sleep in on Saturday morning.

P15 Yep. Sleeping in is fun. I'm wondering what you want to do: Sleep in or play soccer?

T15 Oh, I guess I want to play soccer. No, I know I want to play soccer. But sometimes it's a pain in the neck to get up to go to practice. But if I don't go to practice, I can't play in the game.

P16 You're right. No practice. No game. What do you want to do about it all?

T16 Do you suppose if I came home at 11:30 and went straight to bed that that would work.

P17 After a late snack, but no television? Is that what you're saying?

T17 Yep. What do you think?

P18 11:30 home, snack and off to bed? Sounds OK to me as long as we can avoid that ramming around in the morning before soccer.

T18 OK then. Let's write it on a Post-It and put it on the bulletin board like we did with our plan for the chores.

P19 OK with me. You write it. I'll sign it.

T19 Jeez, Dad, you're always looking for ways to get out of work.

P20 Yep. If I can get you to write it, I'm a happy dad.

T20 What are parents coming to anyhow?

P21 Beats me. Now write that agreement so I can sign it.

Discussion of Parent's Interventions

P1: You never really know when a simple comment will result in Flash Anger. Be prepared for the unexpected.

P2: Parent senses that Kevin's emotional energy is heating up and responds with an I-Message.

P3: Parent's first agreeing statement. What do you think would have happened if the parent had responded, "I don't want any back talk from you, young man, or you're in your room for two weeks?"

P4: A second non-defensive agreeing statement. Kevin is looking for things to argue about because the parent is not giving him anything to "hang" his anger on.

P5: It might sound obvious. But it is better than arguing or fighting fire with fire.

P6: Another agreeing statement.

P7: This is the first inviting criticism intervention. Do you see how Kevin is helped to be more logical and reasonable? There seems to be a slow turn in the direction of a solution.

P8: The non-defensive question helps Kevin to talk about the pictures in his Quality World.

P9: We're on your side, son. Affirmation of the parent/child relationship. The question is another way to help Kevin clarify what is in his Quality World.

P10: The parent asks Kevin to self-evaluate. What do you think would have happened if the parent had said something like this: "You know that idea isn't about to fly in this household. We have rules and we're holding fast to them."

P11: Parent affirms house rules but holds out the possibility of working out a solution to the conflict.

P12: This is a statement of clarification.

P13: Parent affirms the seriousness of the issue for Kevin. And parent voices concern. Parent is telling Kevin about the pictures in the parent's real world.

P14: After all this time, the parent asks Kevin to join in finding a solution to the conflict.

P15: Agreeing statement after the parent sensed an elevation in Kevin's emotional temperature. Parent follows up with asking Kevin what he really wants. What is the more important picture in his Quality World—sleep or soccer?

P16: Parent asks Kevin what Kevin's plan is. Notice that father keeps the responsibility squarely on Kevin's shoulders. The parent is not about ready to come up with a quick fix to get the conflict quickly resolved. The parent is allowing Kevin to struggle.

P17: Clarifying a possible solution.

P18: Parent is clarifying the parental point of view.

P19: Responsibility rests with Kevin.

P20: Humor is safe at this stage of the negotiation. Humor can serve as a release of tension. However, if Kevin's emotional temperature rises, parent will de-fuse with an agreeing statement.

P21: Non-defensive, non-argumentative refocusing to ensure the completion of the problem solving process.

APPENDIX B
An Example of a Husband Managing Wife's Angering

W=Wife's Comments
H=Husband's Interventions

W1: Are you just going to sit there and watch sports all afternoon?

H1: Yep. NCAA basketball time is here and after that the Flyers are playing the Bruins. Ought to be some good games coming up.

W2: That's all you ever do. You just sit there every weekend and watch sports. If it isn't football or basketball it's soccer or something else. Anything but do things with me.

H2: Hey! Whatdaya mean? Did I go with you to your mother's last weekend or did I not? And did I miss the St. John's and Georgetown game because of the visit?

W3: And did you pout and whine for the entire afternoon. No one enjoyed himself or herself because of your moping around.

H3: I did not mope. You're always making things look worse than they are.

W4: How can I make things look worse than they are? Things are "pretty worse" to start with around here.

H4: Ah, you're always blowing everything out of proportion. I'm getting tired of your griping.

W5: I wouldn't always be griping if I got some cooperation from you. All you ever do is think of yourself, the Big Number One. And I mean that if you don't get out of that chair and do some exercise sometime, the Big Number One is going to blow up into a blimp.

H5: You're right. I have gained some pounds in the last year.

W6: Sit in that chair and watch television. That's all you ever do. There's more to life than ESPN.

H6: You're right. There is more to life than watching sports on TV.

W7: You'd never know it from what you do. As soon as you're in that door, flip goes the remote and you're gone.......except for supper which you manage to find time for.

H7: You're absolutely right. I do turn on the TV as soon as I get home.

W8: Well, you would think that a so-called intelligent person like yourself would find something else to do besides being glued to the TV, the idiot box.

H8: OK. You're right. Watching TV isn't all that challenging.

W9: You're right there, Buster.

H9: You really sound burned up at me. No blame intended. I mean that's the way it is right now. But I am interested in understanding how our life would be changed if you had things more the way you wanted them.

W10: I don't know if I could take a chance talking about that with you. You get defensive when I try to talk about what I want.

H10: You're right. I do get defensive. But I read this book about working things out when people are upset, and I realize that my arguing back and being defensive doesn't work.

W11: What book is that and why didn't you read it five years ago when we first got married?

H11: I guess I should have. But we're here in the present now. No kidding, how would you like things to be? I promise not to fight back or try to get revenge.

W12: Well, it is a risk. But....... Well, I just wish we could do more things together.

H12: OK. Like doing what together?

W13: I don't know. Just doing things. Going into the city. Going for walks. I guess just being together......without that ____ television being on.

H13: I'm beginning to get the idea you think that I watch too much television. Joke!

W14: There you go, making fun of me. You never can be serious when I'm trying to talk about something.

H14: My mistake. I apologize. You're right. I should not joke around when we're talking about something important. I think what you are telling me is that you would like to do more together, as a couple. Right?

W15: Well, yes. Isn't that why people get married? They can watch TV by themselves. No, I'm sorry; that shot was uncalled for. You're right. I would like to do more together.

H15: Look, I want to work things out; I mean I do love you and want to keep our marriage alive. Will you join with me and work out a solution that makes things more the way we want them around here?

W16: Well, what if our plan doesn't work out?

H16: We'll keep on trying until we make one that does work.

W17: I don't want to make a plan for being together 24-7. I like my independence, too.

H17: OK. What's one area, one part of our life together we can change to make it more satisfying?

W18: I know you like to watch sports. But can't we do something together on at least one afternoon during the weekend. I mean, get out of here and do something athletic, something that's good for us and good for our physical selves.

H18: Like?

W19: Going for hikes or walks. I love to just walk around in the city. Or hike up in the mountains or walk around the lake. Or play tennis. Just anything as long as we're actively doing something and doing it together.

H19: Sounds OK with me. How do you see it working out? Doing the same thing every weekend, or doing something different each weekend?

W20: What do you think?

H20: I'd like to commit us to Saturday afternoon as our "healthy/togetherness program time." And I think it could be fun to plan and think about it during the week. Then by Thursday or Friday we can decide what we will do on Saturday. It will give us something to look forward to.

W21: Sounds great. When do we start this?

H21: I'm writing this down on paper now: "Jack and Sylvia will spend the time between Saturday 1:00PM and 6:00PM doing things together that will better their minds and bodies. Any outside activity goes. But no TV." What do you say?

W22: OK. Where's the dotted line? I'm ready to sign.

H22: Here you are madam, just sign here and you will be a proud new member of the Saturday Afternoon Health Association. And after we both sign, I'll put the plan on our kitchen bulletin board so neither of us can forget our agreement.

Discussion of Husband's Interventions

H1: He either missed or ignored the heated emotional temperature in the rather barbed question that wife asks.

H2, H3, H4: These are fight-fire-with-fire defensive responses. These are the types of responses to angering messages that often precipitate a real blow-up between husband and wife.

H5: He finally starts to manage the wife's angering by an agreeing statement and does not respond to the personal "shot" which he wife fired off.

H6: Another agreeing message.

H7: Another agreeing message. She's hot and not able to discuss rationally. The helper's job is to de-fuse.

H8: Agreeing once again.

H9: Acknowledgement of wife's anger and an invitation to criticize.

H10: Agreeing and I-Message.

H11: Agreeing and inviting criticism. No You-Messages are allowed here; they would add kindling to the fire.

H12: Essentially, he is saying "No judgment, criticism or blame. Tell me more."

H13: Ill-timed humor. She is not yet in the mood to deal lightly with the issues she is discussing.

H14: He recovered. He apologized, agreed and re-focused the discussion back to his wife's concerns.

H15: Here is the turning point. He is asking her for a shared commitment to work out a solution that is mutually satisfying.

H16: Her emotional temperature is lowered, thus the husband can float an idea and see how it goes. If the wife's emotional temperature rises, he can bring it down by using de-fusing skills.

H17: Here husband is helping the wife to tell him about the pictures in her Quality World.

H18: Tell me more about the pictures in your Quality World.

H19: Tell me more; fill me in on your pictures.

H20: With the emotional energy calm and in a spirit of working together, the husband's ideas can be accepted. If he would have tried this earlier, I'm sure he would have been shot down.

H21,21: Husband is writing the plan, both are signing the plan and the plan is posted.

WORKSHEET ONE

1 What is your definition of "anger?"

2. What are the two "kinds" of anger? Please explain the differences.

3. Identify and describe the four components of "total behavior?"

4. Please explain whether you agree or disagree with this statement: "No one can make me angry. If I anger, angering is my choice."

5. How would you explain the concept of the "Quality World" to a friend?

What are some pictures in your personal Quality World?

6. Can you give four reasons why someone might choose angering behavior to meet their needs?

Can you remember any time in your life when you chose angering behavior to meet your needs? Tell about that situation as you remember it.

7. Do you think angering behavior is bad or good? Please explain.

8. Do you honestly believe that your angering is a behavior you choose? Yes or No?
Please explain your answer.

WORKSHEET TWO

1. Can you remember when you last angered? Was it Flash Anger, Choice Anger or both? How did you know you were angering? How did you manage your angering? Are you pleased with the way you managed your angering?

2. What does the following mean to you? "I cannot blame my angering on anyone else. No one can push my buttons. I am a person and not an elevator."

3. Think of how you have managed your angering behaviors in the past. Since reading this material, have you changed anything about the way you manage your angering? What are the changes you have made?

4. Is it easier for you to change your thinking behavior or your doing behavior? Please explain.

5. Do you believe, "Changing your actions is a powerful and effective key to manage your angering?" Please explain.

6. Have you changed any of your thinking behaviors in order to manage your angering? What thoughts have you changed?

7. Are there pictures in your Quality World that contribute to your angering? How do these pictures conflict with what is going on in your Real World? What actions can you take to resolve the conflict? Is angering a good way to resolve the conflict?

8. What effect does angering have on your personal relationships? Please explain.

9. What are you trying to achieve when you anger? Attention? Control? Avoidance of a painful or fearful situation? Please explain.

10. Do you want to manage your angering differently, or is angering working well for you? Please explain.

WORKSHEET THREE

1. In your own words, please describe the role and functions of a "anger-management helping" person.

2. What is a "therapeutic environment?"
   List the behaviors you can choose in order to create a "therapeutic environment."

3. List any anger "de-fusing" skills that you have found effective.

4. How would you explain "Active Passive Listening" to a friend?

5. What are the two parts to an "Agreeing Statement?"

6.   Do you think it is proper for an adult/parent to send an Agreeing Statement to a youth or teen who is angering at the adult? Please explain your answer.

7.   If you send an "Invitation to Criticize" aren't you showing that you are weak and unsure of yourself? Please explain.

8.   True or False? "After making one or two de-fusing interventions, the angering person can be expected to think and speak logically and rationally." Please explain your answer.

9.   Think of a time when a person Flash Angered at you. Please write an Agreeing Statement and an Inviting Criticism intervention that you could have used to help de-fuse the person.

10. True or False? The skills to manage Flash Angering and Choice Angering are exactly the same. Please explain your answer.

Worksheet Four

1. How do you know when a person is angering and in need of help to manage the angering behavior? What signals do they send?

2. As an anger management helper, what are the two parts of your objective?

3. True or False? When the angering person directs his anger straight at you, there is no way you can help him to cope with his angering. Please explain.

4. Please describe the five steps you can take to help the angering person cope with his angering when the anger is not directly focused on you:

   A.

   B.

   C.

   D.

   E.

5. As helper what is your goal when you are directly involved in the other person's angering?

6. Discuss the six steps the helper can use to assist the angering person to cope when the angering is directed at the helper:

   A.

   B.

   C.

   D.

   E.

   F.

7. In your opinion, what is the most important intervention to carry out when you are trying to help the other person manage his angering? Please explain.

WORKSHEET FIVE

1. True or False? As the anger manager helper, you can expect the angering person to respect your position and be mindful of your feelings, too. Please explain your answer.

2. What steps can you take in your home, office, school or community to prevent angering regardless of the actions or inaction of others? .

3. Please explain the results of using the "Dangerous Five," Angering, Arguing, Blaming, Criticizing, Coercing and Defensing on personal relationships.

4. True or False? When the angering person is de-fused, the helper should show understanding for the angering person's physical and psychological needs by providing

"positive reinforcements" and rewarding the non-anger-ing behavior. Please explain your answer.

5. True or False? As a mature adult and as the helper, you do have control over the angering person's behavior. Therefore, you are in control as to whether he angers or not. Please explain.

6. What is the most important idea you have gained from reading this book? What is the significance of this idea for you?

7. List the actions you plan to take in order to manage the angering you will encounter in the future: Your own and the angering of others.

8. Think of a time when you successfully managed a person's angering behavior. Did you use skills and ideas other than those that were presented in this book? What were the interventions you used? What do you judge was the long-term effect of your anger management on your relationship with the angering person?

BIBLIOGRAPHY

Confer, Charles E. *The Road to Independent Living: Managing Anger—A Workbook for Teenagers.* (1987) King George, VA: American Foster Care Resources.

Confer, Charles E. *Managing Anger: Yours and Mine.* (1985) King George, VA: American Foster Care Resources.

Ellis, Albert *How to Stubbornly Refuse to Make Yourself Miserable About Anything—Yes Anything!* (1988) Secaucus, NJ: Lyle Stuart.

Frankl, Viktor *Man's Search for Meaning* (1959) New York: Washington Square Press.

Glasser, William *Reality Therapy: A New Approach to Psychiatry* (1965) New York: Harper and Row.

Glasser, William Choice Theory: *A New Psychology of Personal Freedom* (1998) New York: Harper and Row.

Glasser, William *Reality Therapy In Action* (2000) New York: Harper and Row.

ABOUT THE AUTHOR

Charles E. Confer, LCSW, ACSW, QCSW, RTC, is Senior Associate of Reality Therapy Associates of Central Pennsylvania. He has held clinical and administrative social work positions in the fields of child welfare, mental health, family and individual counseling and education/training since 1964.

Mr. Confer is a graduate of Bucknell University, Philadelphia Lutheran Theological Seminary and the University of Pittsburgh Graduate School of Social Work. He is a member of the William Glasser Institute, the National Association of Social Workers and the International Foster Care Organization.

Mr. Confer has trained social workers, foster carers and business professionals from the Komi Republic of Russia, through Europe and the Americas, to Honolulu in the Pacific.

He has taught courses on Managing Angry Customers for customer relations staff of Buick, Chevrolet, Toyota of America, Goodyear, Shell of Canada, GM of Canada, H.J. Heinz, Colgate-Palmolive and C&P Telephone. He has served as board member of and consultant to national and international social work organizations.

Mr. Confer lives is Lewisburg, PA, and is available to provide training and consultation. He can be contacted at his email address:

chcon@ptd.net

Arguing
Angering
✳ Blame
✳ Criticism
Coercion
Defensing
Nagging
Complaining

① Say what you see, hear
(info, data, facts)
② Then Express what you
think, feel, believe .